Once Upon A Dream

Poetic Dreams

Edited By Lynsey Evans

First published in Great Britain in 2024 by:

YoungWriters
Est. 1991

Young Writers
Remus House
Coltsfoot Drive
Peterborough
PE2 9BF
Telephone: 01733 890066
Website: www.youngwriters.co.uk

All Rights Reserved
Book Design by Ashley Janson
© Copyright Contributors 2024
Softback ISBN 978-1-83565-483-5
Printed and bound in the UK by BookPrintingUK
Website: www.bookprintinguk.com
YB0592D

FOREWORD

Welcome Reader, to a world of dreams.

For Young Writers' latest competition, we asked our writers to dig deep into their imagination and create a poem that paints a picture of what they dream of, whether it's a make-believe world full of wonder or their aspirations for the future.

The result is this collection of fantastic poetic verse that covers a whole host of different topics. Let your mind fly away with the fairies to explore the sweet joy of candy lands, join in with a game of fantasy football, or you may even catch a glimpse of a unicorn or another mythical creature. Beware though, because even dreamland has dark corners, so you may turn a page and walk into a nightmare!

Whereas the majority of our writers chose to stick to a free verse style, others gave themselves the challenge of other techniques such as acrostics and rhyming couplets.

Each piece in this collection shows the writers' dedication and imagination – we truly believe that seeing their work in print gives them a well-deserved boost of pride, and inspires them to keep writing, so we hope to see more of their work in the future!

CONTENTS

Fulbrook School, Woburn Sands

Athena Koutoula-Byrne (9)	1
Isabella Gadsden (11)	2
Phoebe Mann (10)	4
Robina McLaughlan-Cain (11)	6
Tamzin Christie (10)	7
Bogdan Constantin Mihaila (10)	8
Jake Moore (10)	9
Saskia Heneback (10)	10
Logan Lynch (9)	11
Sienna McLellan (11)	12
Ollie Thompson (10)	13
Teddy Taylor (9)	14
Carson Field (9)	15
Stanley Chapman (10)	16
Sadie Hepton (11)	17
Dexter Jefferies (10)	18

Oakington Manor Primary School, Wembley

Lakshya Lahoti (10)	19
Rim Najm (10)	20
Charlotte Rose Nagle (10)	21
Aarav Dave (10)	22
Aysha Adan (9)	23
Adam Loonat (10)	24
Ivonne Brooke Prodanov (9)	25
Jacob Duarte (10)	26
Punita Tailor (9)	27
Maeda Farhan (9)	28
Zurrell Quaye-Murray (9)	29

Platts Heath Primary School, Platts Heath

Bonnie Crouch (10)	30
Etienne Verwey (10)	31
Sherlock Tang (11)	32
Esther Kettle (11)	33
Scarlett Diamond (9)	34
Henry Sullivan (11)	35
Charlie Gupwell (11)	36

St Charles' Catholic Primary School, Spennymoor

George Gascoigne (11)	37
Leo Armstrong (10)	38
Una Cooper (10)	40
Alex Facey (7)	42
Beau Wilson (11)	44
Zara Charlton (8)	45
Emily Lin (9)	46
Jennifer Saleh (10)	47
Annabelle Bagley (9)	48
Mary Clark (10)	49
Gabriel McCourt (11)	50
Sophie Duggan (8)	51
Lexi Dickinson (11)	52
Henry Bennett (10)	53
Lucy Evans (10)	54
Daniel Smith (9)	55
Tobias Sawyer (10)	56
Eleanor Shaw (10)	57
Neave Fishburn (9)	58
Ella Watts (8)	59
Taylor-Jay Francis (9)	60
Oscar Culey (10)	61

Sadie Gardner (10)	62
Lucas Baker (9)	63
Luca Ajayi (10)	64
Kayden Smith (9)	65
Joe Duggan (8)	66
Ada Wilson (9)	67
Rosie Stephenson (11)	68
Violet Lilly (8)	69
Robyn Lockwood (11)	70
Sebastian Russell (7)	71
Eliza Stanness (10)	72
Samuel Angstmann (11)	73
Jonah Ranyard (10)	74
Martha Brown (8)	75
Sophie Emm (10)	76
Amalie Wilkinson	77
Jack Robinson (8)	78
Kian Arnott (10)	79
Isla Taylor (9)	80
William McMullan (7)	81
Vinny Baker (9)	82
Eryn Turner (9)	83
Summer (8)	84
Heidi Scott (8)	85
Romany Lockwood (8)	86
Emilia Beston (7)	87
Amelia Wade (9)	88
Callum Brown (11)	89
Larna McLeod (8)	90
Finlay Hodgson (11)	91
Harry Glasper (8)	92
Harry Machin (10)	93
Emma Foster (8)	94
Carter Barratt (7)	95
Joel Brown (10)	96
Isaac Ramsay (7)	97
William Armstrong (9)	98
Jake Lim (9)	99
Seb Connor Inchliffe (9)	100
Bertie Corner (8)	101
Sophie-Nicole Hocking (9)	102
Isla Barton (8)	103
Joseph Hall (9)	104
Harris Granger (8)	105
Freya Barratt (7)	106

Winston Way Academy, Ilford

Khadeeja Laheri (7)	107
Ashika Ray (11)	108
Aysha Hassan (8)	109
Riyansh Yadav (9)	110
Zara Mansoor (8)	111
Bhavyesh Bejjam (9)	112
Soraiya Abul (9)	113
Yeshmith Chandanam (8)	114
Shashank Yada (9)	115
Jarin Khan (7)	116
Juhanah Islam (8)	117
Hithesh Chigichorla (8)	118
Yannis Chira (9)	119
Arjun Selvamariappan (10)	120
Ranveer Singh (11)	121
Haram Bhatti (9)	122
Gabrielle Jones-Fletcher (8)	123
Ayaana Alom (8)	124
Aanika Momi (9)	125
Zara Ali (9)	126
Hem Suryansh Kalapala (7)	127
Zuhaib Hassan (9)	128
Shriya Deshpande (10)	129
Siddhi Gannu (8)	130
Amira Islam (8)	131
Rayan Mohammed (7)	132
Alessia Maria (9)	133

THE POEMS

Dragon World

M y dragon world, you will be amazed
Y ou will be surprised, for my dragon world has a dark side

D o stay, there are different types of dragons, so pick your pet and take it home
R aging with fear, the dragons call Batman and Superman
A fter they save the day, we all party
G o on now, don't be shy, come with me in my dragon world
O n we go, a new adventure
N ow we'll be waiting in my dragon world

W ould you bring some friends? Oh, please do,
O ur fun never ends
R ight, off we go, a new day
L uckily, in my dragon land, it never rains
D o come, please do, the fun has just begun.

Athena Koutoula-Byrne (9)
Fulbrook School, Woburn Sands

Dream Or Nightmare?

This vision is boggling my small but mighty mind.
A little seems friendly, a bit is unkind.
How is this possible? Am I overthinking this?
Let me just say, not everything dazzles with bliss.
Pretty pink roses covered in pin-pricking thorns.
Bushes dark as a black hole
With all life on its leaves practically torn.
Yet I swear that I see a glimmer of light
Just a hint, nothing more.
Amongst this land of emptiness, is it real?
I'm not sure.
Miniature patches of perfect green grass
Surround the dull-looking floor.
Flower buds grow in hidden corners
My heart begins to soar.
Still, is this a dream or a nightmare?
It will truly confuse all.
Every clue seems too subtle yet obvious.
Am I making the wrong call?
A sky of stormy grey
Yet it dances like a melody.
Now I must be all wrong.
What is not quickly clear to me?

Wait just a moment,
I may have figured it out!
My eyes pick out the good in bad, without a doubt!
This is a wondrous gift,
It will really take me far.
To some this may seem strange,
But I love how it's bizarre!
I know this is a dream
Telling me everything has a bit of cheer.
You just need to try and make it appear.

Isabella Gadsden (11)
Fulbrook School, Woburn Sands

My Father The Clown

My father was a circus clown,
He liked to play games,
He wasn't insane either, he was sane.
He came home one night,
With red on his shirt,
I asked what it was,
He said it was his fun little flower squirt squirt,
That night, I didn't sleep a wink,
What was that red on his shirt?
I knew it wasn't ink...
Had people been hurt?
No one knew nor wanted to know,
So I set off into the snow,
To the circus to be specific,
All I knew was this was bigger than the Pacific.
My heart stopped faster than a conker hits the ground.
I faced a withered animatronic fox,
His body looked like it survived a million battles.
Then an eagle with an axe for a hand.
And the most terrifying of all,
An animatronic clown which was at least ten feet tall...
A day later, I opened my eyes,
I still saw the roof of the circus,

I felt something hard on my back.
I tried to move a muscle,
But all I heard were cracks,
I at last looked down,
I saw a mountain of bodies,
And the ten-foot clown.
Now I knew what the red was on my father's shirt.

Phoebe Mann (10)
Fulbrook School, Woburn Sands

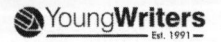

Getting Lost

Getting lost in a book, it is like a dream
Just like when you're eating ice cream

When you open the page you have a feeling that's strange
As powers pull you into your childhood dreams

Little fairies scream to me,
"Come over here and let us see,"

The future lies in our hands and soon we'll need to make a plan
To stop the Earth from being hurt

All around this fairy land I suddenly find a mysterious land
And I come up with a plan

I can see the future is bright
As my father reads me a story and says, "Goodnight."

Robina McLaughlan-Cain (11)
Fulbrook School, Woburn Sands

I'm Dreading The Summer

I'm dreading the summer holidays,
Because then I'll have to leave,
My favourite place in the whole wide world,
And Hogwarts is its name.

Hogwarts is like a castle,
But it's glorious in every way,
From its solid marble floors,
To its dark stone roofs.

I love all the houses as well,
But I think mine is the best,
Because Ravenclaws are full of wit and wisdom,
And we don't dare fail in tests.

That's why I'm dreading the summer,
Because Hogwarts is brilliant,
Hogwarts is the...
Best!

Tamzin Christie (10)
Fulbrook School, Woburn Sands

The Day Was Snowy...

We didn't have any food,
So we went to kill cows,
But wolves were coming.

The fear I had, no one knew.
I just went home.
Nobody was there...

The wolves were here,
I was devastated,
I asked for help,
But nobody came...

Then, one day,
Somebody came,
But they left,
And left me forever.

Snakes were coming,
But at the last moment,
I woke up in the blackness.

It was 3 in the morning,
But I then was still scared,
Because I would have that bizarre dream.

Bogdan Constantin Mihaila (10)
Fulbrook School, Woburn Sands

The Dark Alleyway

As I walked down the alleyway
Lonely as can be
I saw darkness there, waiting for me.
My instincts told me to run,
But you can't escape darkness
It always won.

Tap tap, tap tap, tap tap,
Was all I could hear
In the dark night
I was filled with fear.

As I opened my eyes
I was back on earth,
I thought it was all a daydream
Until I saw a shiny beam.

Tap tap, tap tap.
I found myself running again.
Bang, bang!
Was it a gun
Or a very scared one?

Jake Moore (10)
Fulbrook School, Woburn Sands

Animal Kingdom

Soaring up a mile high,
In the darkness,
In the sky,
Feathers on my wings in the air,
Higher than a group of stairs,
Inky stars in the night,
This is my moonlit flight.

Climbing high in my tree,
Chittering out my biggest dreams,
Tail swinging everywhere,
Leaves all stuck in my hair.

Looking cute in my tree,
There's no one quite like me,
I am the softest in the zoo,
And I'm sure you'll love me too,
From Australia, fluffy and sweet,
Koalas rule, it's quite the treat!

Saskia Heneback (10)
Fulbrook School, Woburn Sands

The Dragon!

In my dream,
I am floating towards a cave
With spiderwebs.
Deep in the cave,
I see a flashing light,
And a hear a big and mighty roar!

I walk in the cave and see
A big, mighty dragon,
With teeth as sharp as a knife,
Claws as big as a treasure chest.
The dragon is as big as
A six-storey skyscraper,
And it breathes fire out of its nose.

All of a sudden,
The dragon sees me.
I run, and it chases me,
But I stop, and it stops,
And we become best friends,
With the dragon.

Logan Lynch (9)
Fulbrook School, Woburn Sands

Fairies On The Run

Prepare for your brains to be frazzled and cooked alive,
As you will never find us, no matter where we hide!

We hide in the day and come out at night,
You can never see us no matter where we fly.

In the night we sing our terrible songs,
That will make your nightmares sing along.

We live in trees which you might not expect,
But we look just like you too.

We're so tiny, flying around,
You will never find us when you wake from your dreams,
You will never know where we've been!

Sienna McLellan (11)
Fulbrook School, Woburn Sands

The Creature In The Alleyway

Down in the alleyway where I shall be
Down in the alleyway where darkness shall be
Down in the alleyway where it shall be waiting for me

One day, I ran into the forest (I was playing hide-and-seek)
I hid and hid
And hid and hid...
But no one found me but it did

Down in the alleyway where I faced it again
It stood in front of me, I wanted to run and cry
But the pain wouldn't let me,
I stood as scared as could be.
I shed a painful tear as it grabbed me
And pulled me in.

Ollie Thompson (10)
Fulbrook School, Woburn Sands

The Painting

T he time we got curious
H eat of fire in our body
E ven though it was dangerous we went.

P assion and strength were key
A fter rummaging around we found it
I n we went to the painting
N othing was stopping us
T he shadow hid something
I n the blink of an eye, something came
N ow our hearts were beating
"G o," it said and I woke up in my bed.

Teddy Taylor (9)
Fulbrook School, Woburn Sands

Dreams And Nightmares

D eath all around me
R outine every day
E at and sleep
A rmy warzone
M edic healing the hurt.

N eedles from doctors
I njuries and wounds
G uns and saws
H atred and anger
T ickled half to death
M eteors exploding
A steroids hitting Earth
R ain thudding down
E lephants stamping.

And that's how dreams end.

Carson Field (9)
Fulbrook School, Woburn Sands

My World

It's different in my world
Pigs all around
Footballs are living
And stories are told
My friends laughing
And I'm all old
The time is unlimited
Chocolate is too
When you eat it
You'll need the loo
My world is fantastic
Hope you'll see
My world is great
Just like me!

Stanley Chapman (10)
Fulbrook School, Woburn Sands

A Dream

A dream that only one can see,
It's much more than your imagination.
It's your childhood where
All your dreams become real.

You shut your eyes and count to ten,
And your dreams become real.
You see all the things you imagined.
Today you see the winged bear,
Or the crocodile bird.

Sadie Hepton (11)
Fulbrook School, Woburn Sands

The Figure

I was in a library in a haunted hotel
With glowing cracks in the walls
I was all alone
It was like the hotel was alive.

But the point is
I was free to do whatever I want.

Dexter Jefferies (10)
Fulbrook School, Woburn Sands

The Bridge To The Future

A portal arose in the sky one day,
Swirling, twisting, twirling like a spinning spiral,
I chose a daring choice and leapt through,
It seemed as if time had sprinted through a century.

As I emerged, the revolving mass of light vanished,
My eyes were amazed to catch a glimpse of,
The landscape around me, I was in the year 2124!

Towering, plexiglass skyscrapers loomed over me,
Conjoined by levitating, hanging bridges,
Speedy maglevs zoomed across the megapolis,
Controlled by magnets, fastening the train into place.

I peeked through the impenetrable glass,
There were extendable tables, reclining beds,
And most surprising of all, which I was green with envy,
A bookcase that turned to see a high-quality TV.

Lakshya Lahoti (10)
Oakington Manor Primary School, Wembley

Prestigious Audition

All I hear are sounds of delight,
"Oh me?"
I tremble in fear I'm doing nothing fine,
Anonymous people flying like birds,
Ballerinas spinning and twirling continuously with smirks in their eyes,
A choir of singers chant until the birds fly,
The population of people gazing with all of their sight,
Twirling, twisting and turning, the stage's amazement is bright,
The money they want is to fight for,
Death stares of disapproval mutter from my right,
My technique, and my choreography are not right,
The lights flicker like fireflies,
Determined dancers' routines formally organised,
A flicker of hope I'm imagining in my mind,
My shoes were dancing without me with a terrible sign,
The dollar signs keep circling in my head,
I'm guessing that this is the finish line,
The light above reveals the winning sign,
An unknown dance I accomplish with hope,
I impressed them, oh yes, I am the winning girl,

Rim Najm (10)
Oakington Manor Primary School, Wembley

Dragon Dreams

D ivine creatures gliding across the sky,
R oaring and growling at me,
A ctive volcanoes forming a lava sea,
G leaming at me is the blinding yellow sun,
O n the dragons I perch, riding them is fun,
N othing can stop me now, I hope this dream is never done.

D efying gravity, like a helium balloon,
R eally high up I went,
E xtraordinary heights I reached while on this dragon,
A ll of a sudden I fell, screeching at the top of my lungs,
M adly I shouted, "Help me!"
S adly it was no use, I fell to my death...

Charlotte Rose Nagle (10)
Oakington Manor Primary School, Wembley

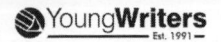

The Masked Person...

In my dreams every night,
I take a step foward onto the field.
The fog concealed a person,
A masked person holding a knife.
A grin appeared on its face,
There was no escape.
Its eye glowed bright red, only seeking blood,
Like a raging bull it chased me.
The bag on my shoulder was all I had,
I threw the bag, slowing it down.
I tried to climb a fence,
But it never ended.
The beast shook the fence,
I fell...
The creature held the knife, facing me,
I closed my eyes.
I woke up safe at home in my bed,
The mattress felt wet, I wonder why?

Aarav Dave (10)
Oakington Manor Primary School, Wembley

Emerald Green Northern Lights Queen

Aurora Borealis, gorgeous galaxy queen.
As she twists and turns in her stunning dress,
Around the Earth's axis.

Aurora Borealis; people look at her in awe,
Wondering what she holds:
An oyster filled with pearls,
A vault drowning in money,
Or a treasure chest coughing up gold.
Whatever she holds, beauty follows.

Aurora Borealis, the highlight of our nights,
She brings nothing but pure delight.

Aysha Adan (9)
Oakington Manor Primary School, Wembley

Jurassic World

As I sleep at night,
I dream of a world filled with enormous dinosaurs.
Armed with sharp teeth,
They hunt their prey.
As I allow myself to explore,
I become excited a lot more.
I see predators devouring their scrumptious prey,
I hear the roars of T-rexes.
I smell dead meat about to be consumed,
And as I turn around,
A predator chases me to my death.
I then wake up to see,
It was only a dream!

Adam Loonat (10)
Oakington Manor Primary School, Wembley

My Creative World

Every night, I lie in bed,
And drift off to sleep.
In my mind,
I hear, "Ready for take off."

And there I arrive in a world,
Where creativity has no limits,
The architecture is magnificent.
You can only feel good vibes.

Oh my,
I never want this dream to end,
But I feel someone shaking my head.
I hope I'm lucky to continue
My dream again!

Ivonne Brooke Prodanov (9)
Oakington Manor Primary School, Wembley

Race Cars

R eady for races at any moment
A mazing superstars drifting through the course
C an drive at amazing speeds
E nthusiastic to their job

C razy people driving at the speed of light
A ggressive when driving
R evving their engines
S pectacular skills on the track.

Jacob Duarte (10)
Oakington Manor Primary School, Wembley

Unicorns

U nicorns dancing in the night sky
N ight skies full of unicorns
I see their dances and prances
C ollaborating in unity
O ver the stars they dance
R iding on the path of the moonlight
N o unicorn is left behind
S o majestic, they decorate the sky.

Punita Tailor (9)
Oakington Manor Primary School, Wembley

Dreams Take You To The Right Place!

D reams can be full of ups and downs.
R ealistically you might get nightmares.
E ven though dreams can be good they lead to nightmares!
A larming ghosts haunt your dreams.
M ortifying monsters leaping under your bed!
S uddenly you wake... phew!

Maeda Farhan (9)
Oakington Manor Primary School, Wembley

Slumber Sleep

S atisfaction, everyone needs to develop their minds,
L eap into your dreams to discover the future you,
E njoy your slumber sleep while you can,
E xcellent sleep gets you magnificent grades,
P arty during the sleep and go deep into the dream.

Zurrell Quaye-Murray (9)
Oakington Manor Primary School, Wembley

Monsters Make Horrors

Are you there? Turn the lights off
To see me appear
Monster in the closet, so you're right
Watching you sleep all night
Wherever you sleep; I'm known as the creep
You try to escape, I'm still here
Flying beside you, wearing a cape
I'm here, in the ceiling
I'm appealing
Watching your every move
Under the moonlight
Feeling a groove
You leave for school
It's a miracle
I'm free
I know you're Lee
It's obvious
I watch you sleep
I watch you gleep
You grow up
I fly and say goodbye.

Bonnie Crouch (10)
Platts Heath Primary School, Platts Heath

The Stairs

This is a crazy dream so buckle up.
It started by getting greeted by Nanny Barbara.
At dinner, we sat down and ate, when I took a bite, it screamed and ran away.
My family was confused but I went upstairs.

In the middle of the night, I was hungry
So I went to get a snack, I went down but I heard a
crash, bang, crack,
Then I saw a dead Nanny.

Her spine sticking out of her back, I only wanted a snack.

Her head on the door handle and her toes on a candle.

Her nose filled with snot, she looked like a special robot.

Etienne Verwey (10)
Platts Heath Primary School, Platts Heath

No One In The World!

Wake in the bed.
No one out there.

Slithering off the bed.
Just like a snake.

He called his mum.
But no one out there.
Outside the day is so grey.
Just like today with no one there.

He goes to school as usual.
But he still can't see anyone.

He walks to everywhere he knows.
Still no one there.
Suddenly, he knows there are no more people in this world.

He wakes up from the dream.
When everything is back.
He knows it's just a dream.

Sherlock Tang (11)
Platts Heath Primary School, Platts Heath

The Mouse And Mole Fighting For Cheese

The mouse runs through the small, tiny hole
Oh my gosh, what's that? A very fat mole
Let's hope you're not scared of blood
If you are then I'll just have to throw you in the mud
Woah, look at all that cheese
I feel spiders crawling up my knees
All that cheese is mine, not yours
The mouse gets so angry that he just roars
Aargh, a massive mole
Aargh, a massive mouse
What's that? I hear screaming
The big bright sun is beaming.

Esther Kettle (11)
Platts Heath Primary School, Platts Heath

Daydream

Oh so similar, but so different
When you are bored I play,
Mind games is where I wish to stay.
I've always been a friend until I'm not
When you realise you had a plan
I ruin it.
Stare out the window, you will find me
Not when you're asleep
Rather when you're lively and awake.
Wide awake I can put you in a wonderland
Or your worst fear,
But it's you who makes me appear.
I am a daydream.

Scarlett Diamond (9)
Platts Heath Primary School, Platts Heath

I Just Wanted A Snack

Once upon a dream,
Sat a boy on a sofa,
Wondering what would happen,
When you fall downstairs.

He jumps from his attic stairs,
Falling from the top to the very bottom,
He stands up at first,
But then falls to the floor.

His parents notice and are very,
Very shocked and mad,
But he said,
"I totally just wanted a snack."

Henry Sullivan (11)
Platts Heath Primary School, Platts Heath

Stuck In A Dream

Stuck in a dream,
No one to be seen,
When he found out,
He tried to get out.

Every exit was blocked with only a door locked.

He stared at someone,
Someone stared at him,
He smiled amazingly,
He smiled gracefully,
The walls are as white as snow,
He gave a sigh with a bow.

Charlie Gupwell (11)
Platts Heath Primary School, Platts Heath

Astronaut

A ll my dreams come true as I look out of the spaceship window.
S parkly stars appear as the Earth disappears, striking, striking away from me.
T winkling like diamonds in cosmic space, I see terror in my astronaut reflection in the window.
R ocks from an asteroid fly close, rumbling and ricocheting our rocket ship.
O uch! We've been hit. Oh, no! A rock has struck the spaceship.
N ot only that, but it's damaged a fuel tank and we have lost control.
A s if by magic, we see lights ahead. Could it be aliens on an alien spaceship?
U nited as one, they respond to our mayday signals. United, they understand my morse code flashes from my torch.
T ogether, we are guided safely back to Earth. Together, we wave goodbye. Together, we sigh with relief; we are safe. Then my alarm clock starts to play music. I wake up suddenly and stare out of my window. I see lights in the sky. Together, we are astronauts!

George Gascoigne (11)
St Charles' Catholic Primary School, Spennymoor

Untitled

As I drifted off to sleep in my comfy bed
A great big pirate ship popped up in my head
The ship was old and wooden with a massive skull sail
I think they were trying to get us
To pinch our treasure trail
The pirate stood on top of the ship
He had a patch on his eye and a big chunky lip
He had long straggly hair and a hook for a hand
He looked through his telescope and he could see the land
This was the island that had the treasure chest
We better get there before the rest
Mam put your foot down, we need to be fast
We are in a race and don't want to be last
In the distance, I could see something shiny
Sticking out of the sand, it was the box of treasure
The pirate had it in his hand
We jumped out of the boat hoping we would float
Then all of a sudden a supersonic dolphin shoved us onto his fin
To the treasure to help us win
He went straight through the sand and made a hole

The pirate fell in and went down a well
We grabbed the chest and had a rest with the dolphin's family.

Leo Armstrong (10)
St Charles' Catholic Primary School, Spennymoor

Dreams

In my land of dreams, where my wishes come alive,
My imagination takes a joyful dive,
With eyes wide open and full of hope,
One sets sail on a magical boat,
Through fluffy clouds and sparkling stars,
I begin to explore a world that's far,
Giant teddy bears and talking trees,
Whisper secrets in the warm breeze,
In my dreamland colours dance and sing,
As fairies flutter their magnificent wings,
Unicorns prance on rainbows high,
While giggling mermaids swim nearby,
My dream takes me to exotic places unknown,
Where millions of candies and chocolate are grown,
With each step, the world becomes more grand,
And my imagination expands,
But as my dream nears its end,
Now it is time to ascend,
With a smile on my face and my heart full of glee,
I wake up knowing my dreams will always be free,
So let us cherish the dreams we hold dear,
For in them, possibilities are crystal clear,

Our dreams are a precious thing,
A world of wonder that makes hearts sing.

Una Cooper (10)
St Charles' Catholic Primary School, Spennymoor

Moonlight Chase

I'm running through the forest, the moon lights my path.
I can hear my heart beating and my breath heaving fast.

Heavy footsteps are behind me, my feet are thudding on the ground.
I turn around to see who's there, but no figure to be found.

I try a call for help - is there anyone to save me?
But no matter how hard I try, my voice is stuck inside me.

Glowing eyes are in the bushes, an owl watches me run by.
The snap of a twig sends him up into the night sky.

One last dash for safety, I don't seem to be getting home.
I want to be safe in my bed - not in this forest all alone.

The sound of panting behind me - I trip over my feet!
I close my eyes tightly, the branch above me creaks.

The fierce creature wags his tail and jumps up onto my bed.
I wake up with him licking my face - no longer filled with dread.

Alex Facey (7)
St Charles' Catholic Primary School, Spennymoor

Footballing Fantasy Full Of Fantastic Adventures

F inally, I drift away into my dreams, but strangely, what is about to happen feels wildly real.

O MG, my heart was racing like a cheetah. It was Mary Earps, and she asked me to play football with her.

O ur team was winning. On our team, we had Mary in goal and myself on the wing. The rest of our team was made up of dragons.

T he crowd went wild, roaring with glee, literally, as they were dragons.

B eing small, all of the dragons were able to lift me up off the floor and fly me around the mythical land.

A round the magical place were all sorts of different creatures. There were massive monsters, big blobs, unique unicorns, fantastic fairies and more.

L egends that we thought couldn't be real had happened all in one night; it was wonderful.

L oads of things have gone on in one night. Was it a dream, or could it be real?

Beau Wilson (11)
St Charles' Catholic Primary School, Spennymoor

Enchanted Utopia

I walk barefoot along the grass
Where specks of water glisten like glass
An enchanted oasis all around
Where butterflies glide and birds sound
I hear pitter-patter of hooves from afar
It catches my attention like a shooting star
With a glimpse of a mane and a swish of a tail
A unicorn flies and glides like a boat's sail
A snow-white beast canters through the land
As softly as footprints in the sand
I hear gentle buzzing near my face
As fairies play like they're in a race
I close my eyes to remember this forever
A time never to be forgotten is my endeavour
The sound of children's laughter fills the air
Likened to enjoyment at a summer funfair
Leaving this wonderful land with memories I adore
Hoping and praying I experience this once more.

Zara Charlton (8)
St Charles' Catholic Primary School, Spennymoor

Pink Fluffy Unicorns

P ink fluffy unicorns
I n my dreams, their fur is like thorns
N aughty unicorns dancing on rainbows
K nights are their biggest foes

F lying across the skies
L anding in apple pies
U nicorns, they are like the biggest pests
F amous for putting people's patience to the test
F oolish unicorns can be slow
Y et you can accidentally stub your toe

U nicorns don't like not being fed
N ext time when you want to pet a unicorn don't just go ahead
I nstead back away with caution
C ause they might eat a portion
O f your finger
R ight now they like to linger
N ow be careful
S oon they will try to trick you with a jewel.

Emily Lin (9)
St Charles' Catholic Primary School, Spennymoor

My Magic Movie Theatre

At 8pm,
All tucked up and cosy,
My lights switched off.
I start to feel dozy.
I never fuss when my parents say it's time for bed
Because I know something special is waiting in my head.
I've arrived as always in my comfy chair
With my popcorn, my blanket and my little teddy bear.
The screen has started to glow a sparkling purply blue.
I jump out of my chair and wonder what to do.
I've been sucked into a magical movie land
Where I quest with Harry Potter
And hold a wand in my hand.
I have a snack with the Minions,
A banana split.
We fight over the bananas but the Minions win it.
Tonight has been the best.
It was so much fun, but it ended with the beeping of my annoying alarm
Beep, beep, it goes as sunshine floods my face,
I wonder what's on tonight at my favourite place!

Jennifer Saleh (10)
St Charles' Catholic Primary School, Spennymoor

The Knight's Quest

Once upon a time, in a land far away,
Where magical creatures frolic and play,
There lived a brave knight, strong and true,
On a quest for a fairy tale just for you.

In a mystical forest, dark and deep,
A hidden treasure, secrets to keep,
A princess trapped in a tower so high,
Awaiting a hero with the courage to fly.

With a gleaming sword and armour bright,
The knight embarked on a daring fight.
Through enchanted lands, he journeyed on,
To rescue the princess, his heart's song.

He faced dragons fierce and witches sly,
But never once did he question why,
For love and honour guided his way,
To bring light to the darkness, come what may.

Annabelle Bagley (9)
St Charles' Catholic Primary School, Spennymoor

Flowers In The Meadow

Flowers growing in the meadow,
Fairies dancing around them in circles,
And so we went to go and see if we could help,
Me and my best friend wanted to explore,
In the distance, the fairies saw us,
And came to investigate us,
"Run away," squeaked the fairies. "The giants are here."
They scrambled away,
In a second we realised what the fairies were doing,
And we called them and said,
"Come back, we want to help you grow flowers,
And make the world a better place!"
Embarrassed the fairies said we could help,
And we could get to work right away!
So we all grew flowers happily, and
Now the bees live there!

Mary Clark (10)
St Charles' Catholic Primary School, Spennymoor

A Midwinter Night's Dream

One night, I fell into a deep, deep sleep,
And in my dreams heard the animals speak.
I could understand every word that was said,
As I lay dreaming in my bed.

They told a story of long, long ago,
Of how the dinosaurs arrived here in UFOs.
They did wondrous things while on their trip,
They even built the pyramids of ancient Egypt.
The Grand Canyon was fun to dig out of the ground,
And they built mountains and rivers all around.

But time soon passed by as they knew that it would,
And off they flew to the bright skies for good.
When I woke in the morning on that nice sunny day,
I thought of them out there in the vast Milky Way.

Gabriel McCourt (11)
St Charles' Catholic Primary School, Spennymoor

Magical Dancers

M agical dancers entering the stage
A udience watching
G irls spinning and twirling full of magic
I ncredible scenes as the magic begins
C heerful crowds clapping and shouting
A mazing dancers being magical
L uminous lights bright and sparkling

D ancing bright full of delight
A ll happy and free under the light
N oise so loud as the dancers prance
C arefully moving and shaking as they dance
E xit the stage as they rise to fame
R eady to leave as the crowd calls their name
S upreme dreams of dancing with pretty girls and boys prancing.

Sophie Duggan (8)
St Charles' Catholic Primary School, Spennymoor

The Enchanted Realm

In a land beyond the mortal sight,
Where the moonbeams dance with the night,
Lies a realm of magic unfold.

Through misty woods and ancient trees,
Whispers float upon the breeze,
Of fairy folk and noble knights,
Bound by ancient mystic rites.

Dragons soar across the sky,
Their scales gleaming, fierce and high,
Guarding treasures rich and rare,
In caverns hidden, beyond compare.

Wizards weave their spells of old,
In towers tall with secret bold,
Their magic sparks the midnight air,
A symphony beyond compare.

In this realm where dreams take flight,
Hope and wonder burn so bright.

Lexi Dickinson (11)
St Charles' Catholic Primary School, Spennymoor

The Call Of The Beast

Deep in sleep, I heard a noise,
Was it a roar, and where did it come from?
Wait, was it a plane? A dragon? Or was it a dog?
I looked, and I listened, but nothing was there,
So the sound I followed.

Through jungles, I ran,
In and out of bushes.
On my way to find the source
Of the noise that convinced me to follow.
The call of the beast.

As I got nearer and nearer,
The noise of the beast got louder and louder,
Until I saw it!
It was a dragon.
It glared at me and then
It opened its mouth and
Boom!
I was awake again
And wondering what had happened.

Henry Bennett (10)
St Charles' Catholic Primary School, Spennymoor

Sweet Dream

Swirling, whirling down a swimming pool,
It was quite scary but mostly cool.
When I hit the ground with a bump,
My mind went blank, and my heart thumped.
I opened my eyes to see a world of wonder,
The sight was even more powerful than thunder.
There were lollipop trees,
And dark chocolate bees.
There were candyfloss clouds,
And small crowds of Jelly Tot cows.
When I looked to my right,
I got a huge fright.
I saw a small walking teddy bear,
All I could do was stare.
The teddy bear said, "A merry berry piece of pleasure,
The amount of chocolate we surely can't measure."

Lucy Evans (10)
St Charles' Catholic Primary School, Spennymoor

Once Upon A Dream

A dream, a dream,
An ageless, timeless world without end
Full of colour and small, cute, cuddly animals
How great it is.

A dream, a dream, a world of wonder
Where you can climb the highest mountain or land on Mars.
You can explore the deepest sea and
Can shake hands with a friendly robot dolphin.

A dream, a dream, a world without end,
Where you could end all war,
Find a cure for cancer
Or even be a great Norse god like Thor.

A dream, a dream, is a place
Where happiness and sadness can be at the same time.
A dream for everyone is all the same
And that is unique.

Daniel Smith (9)
St Charles' Catholic Primary School, Spennymoor

Dinosaurs

D uring the night I have a dream, of a dinosaur so loud I scream.
I take a step closer and see, that the dinosaur is nice as can be.
N ow I see more, a dinosaur of every shape and size coming out to roar.
O n the hill, I see the biggest of them of all, it cannot be!
S o it is towering above them all, a Titanosaur, loud and tall.
A nd then I realise where I am, the age of the dinosaur I thought had passed,
U nder my feet, the grounds begin to rumble, as dinosaurs stamped with their wildest dreams,
R ight then they were free, without knowing what was soon to be.

Tobias Sawyer (10)
St Charles' Catholic Primary School, Spennymoor

Dream

When I fall asleep, I dream sweet dreams.
I go downstairs, look in the fridge and eat everything in sight.
I munch, munch, munch until I'm filled with my lunch.
I fly upstairs, open my snack drawer and eat, eat, eat.
I look around to see I am alone.
I jump on the couch, I jump on the bed,
I jump on everything except for my new bed.
I think about rainbows, unicorns and especially clouds.
I wish I was riding a unicorn over the clouds.
Up in the sky is where I go.
Up in my head is where I think instead.
My dream comes to an end so that's
Night, night, sweet dreams for me.

Eleanor Shaw (10)
St Charles' Catholic Primary School, Spennymoor

Tea With My Mam

I went out for tea with my mam,
I ordered a large pizza topped with ham,
The bar lady was very nice, she topped my glass with lots of ice,

The pub was very busy and loud,
The football was playing on TV,
It brought in quite the crowd,

We sat on table one,
After the match people had gone,

The seats were comfy and the backs were high,
I felt like I could touch the sky,

After my tea I felt rather full,
The sky was dark and dull,
It was time to go home to bed,
Mam tucked me in with my favourite ted.

Neave Fishburn (9)
St Charles' Catholic Primary School, Spennymoor

My Hopes And Dreams

I dream I live a happy life with my friends and family
I dream I will become a vet where I will make animals feel better
But I am not always sure what I want to do
Maybe I will work in a zoo
And help an animal or two
I hope I can help all animals in need
That would be the greatest deed
I often dream I met a pony called Tony
Who loved macaroni
And he would show me his friends
And at that moment I saw them
My eyes lit up with joy
But the moment I wake up I realise it's all just a dream
Not all as it seemed...

Ella Watts (8)
St Charles' Catholic Primary School, Spennymoor

Night Light

It's dark and it's creepy up in my room,
The wind is whistling a scary tune,
But I have a night light which saves me from my fears,
I drift off to sleep, to a land with no meaning,
I see a big manor house with a red door that's flaming,
I'm drawn to the handle, I open it, and then,
I take a big step forward but no flooring is there,
I fall through the darkness, and land with a thud,
I open my eyes, the night light is flickering,
It was all just a dream,
I'm guided by the night light to my bed once more.

Taylor-Jay Francis (9)
St Charles' Catholic Primary School, Spennymoor

Insomnia

I n bed, you can't sleep while the monsters creep.
N ightmares, night after day, ruin your sleep and keep you awake.
S oon, you're in bed, you fear the monsters are getting near.
O nce it's morning, you shout hooray but fear another day.
M orning comes once again, you always will remember when the monsters are coming near.
N o one is near, when you should fear is here.
I nside your mind, there is no escape.
A fter all, there is nothing to be scared of just a nightmare. Or is it?

Oscar Culey (10)
St Charles' Catholic Primary School, Spennymoor

On The Clouds

My dream
Was supreme
I was on the clouds
Just above town
I was with all my toys
Without a noise
It was like I could fly
To lift my feet and touch the sky
I look below and I don't want to go
However, if the clouds could carry two
I hope I can fly with you
As I wave down below
I can see the tears build up in your eyes
But everyone has to say goodbye
I can see people's sadness
And they need a bit of joy
So I sprinkle a bit of
Love, happiness and positivity
To their day.

Sadie Gardner (10)
St Charles' Catholic Primary School, Spennymoor

Dreams

Sometimes when you're
Having a dream you might,
Wake up and you might just scream
When you go to bed you might use
Your head and maybe think
Of the colour red,
When you go to sleep you could hear a sheep
Or maybe you could hear a
Really loud beep
When you sleep at night
You might imagine you are
In a fight
You might think you are
On a kite
While you bite
When your head is on a
Cushion you might think
Of a big red button, you
Might think you can fly high
To the sky!

Lucas Baker (9)
St Charles' Catholic Primary School, Spennymoor

The Tall Man

I closed my eyes and drifted to sleep,
Suddenly, I was transported to the deep,
I looked to my side,
And there was a tall man next to me.
I wondered who he was but I carried on through the deep,
He scared me, I won't tell a lie,
But we carried on, side by side.
I could only see his eyes and his wide great smile.
I really wanted to wake from my sleep,
And then he took my hand and made me feel safe,
In this horrible wretched place,
At last, I woke from my slumber,
My nightmare was now over.

Luca Ajayi (10)
St Charles' Catholic Primary School, Spennymoor

Dragon Dreams

I close my eyes and imagine I am in the skies
A tall beast
Big and wide
And gigantic, monstrous jaw
I've looked inside.

With teeth as yellow as a mustard swamp
I need to look out for his crocodile bite and chomp.

His roar is as loud as an earthquake rumble
He can even make one city crumble.

We zoom around like an F16 fighter jet.
He is happy that we have met.

I wish I could stay in this beautiful dream
I wake up in my bed
Things aren't what they seem.

Kayden Smith (9)
St Charles' Catholic Primary School, Spennymoor

Joe's Dream Team

Joe wanted a football team
First, he needed players to pick his first eleven
Pelé, Zidane and Messi all made it into the team
Joe needed one more player, someone who was quick
He saw Ronaldo standing there in his kit

There is no cheating as Joe is the referee
There are no mega wages and the transfers are free
The games are live on TV, you don't have to subscribe
The players never take a dive

The crowd is big and noisy
Every time they score a goal they roar the team so loud.

Joe Duggan (8)
St Charles' Catholic Primary School, Spennymoor

Once Upon A Wizard

W hen I close my eyes, I see a wizard sitting there waiting for me.
I follow him round and he shows me flying fish, jumping jaguars and dancing dogs.
Z igzagging through the air, the wind in my hair, lots of people look up and stare.
A quick flash of colour in my eye, we go down to the ground.
R unning around, I realise I need to go home.
D own the path, I go up a hill, I weave around a flour mill and in a flash, I am back home and beginning to moan as my mother tells me to get up.

Ada Wilson (9)
St Charles' Catholic Primary School, Spennymoor

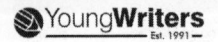

A Netballer's Dream

In my dreams every night,
I dream about an amazing sight,
All around me,
Everyone is as quiet as can be,
As they try to see what is happening,
I stand right here,
With arms in the air,
Trying to push back my hair,
As I need a clear shot to get the ball through the net,
While I throw the ball up high,
My hopes rocket into the sky,
This game needs to end on a high,
When the whistle blows the ball goes through,
And I know I have done what I needed to.

Rosie Stephenson (11)
St Charles' Catholic Primary School, Spennymoor

Dream Land

D reams from a land I've never seen before
R ivers of gold with purple, sandy shores
E legant pegasi fly through the red sky
A nd chase each other going very high
M ajestic, tall, teal trees dancing in the wind

L eaves that are orange, whispering to the mind
A dventures are waiting to be discovered in this land
N o room for nightmares because they are banned
D ream ends, waiting to be entered again.

Violet Lilly (8)
St Charles' Catholic Primary School, Spennymoor

World Of Magic!

In my dream,
People fly on broomsticks,
Many people love to befriend fairies,
Dragons, unicorns and trolls are all real,
We use special potions to hide us from pirates,
All of us are friendly and loving to each other,
Wands have granted us special powers for centuries now,
Dragons fly high with unicorns past sparkling rainbows,
In my dream, you can walk on rainbows,
Every night in my dream, me and my friends walk on rainbows while eating magical popcorn.

Robyn Lockwood (11)
St Charles' Catholic Primary School, Spennymoor

Dreamscape

D arkness comes, time to sleep
R est your eyes, not a peep
E nter Sandman, bring my dreams
A ll an illusion, not as it seems
M agic and mystery, wonder and awe
S omewhere in my slumber, I've been here before
C astles and rainbows, shooting stars
A nimals and creatures from near and far
P owers in my head, to dream of wonderful things
E arly morning comes, my alarm bell rings.

Sebastian Russell (7)
St Charles' Catholic Primary School, Spennymoor

When I Am Older

When I grow up I want to be a pirate,
Hoping I get to sail the sea,
Every day exploring worlds, being free,
Never knowing where I'll be.

I dream of being the best first mate in history.

Attacking villages with our swords,
My fellow pirates celebrate victory.

Oh, I dream of being a pirate someday,
Looking for gold and treasure,
Every day is full of mystery,
Riding on the waves leading us to our treasure.

Eliza Stanness (10)
St Charles' Catholic Primary School, Spennymoor

Drumming Dream

I often find myself dreaming about,
Crowds of fans who scream and shout.
Rather than being a chef or a plumber,
I am a rockstar and a world-class drummer.
Bigger than The Beatles, louder than Queen,
The most spectacular rock band the world has ever seen.
The crowd's clapping and shouting my name,
My drumming and beats leading to fame.
Filling Wembley and travelling with my band,
The dreams for my future are exciting and grand.

Samuel Angstmann (11)
St Charles' Catholic Primary School, Spennymoor

My Dream Is Everybody Gets Along

It would be good if everyone got along,
But sadly, that isn't the case.
In other countries, like Ukraine,
People are fighting, and we need to stop this,
We can help by being kind to all the human race.

This fighting needs to stop,
No matter what,
We can bring peace to the world,
By starting small but like a little baby,
Peace will eventually grow tall,
If we show kindness.
This is my dream to end all worry.

Jonah Ranyard (10)
St Charles' Catholic Primary School, Spennymoor

Astronaut

A stronaut travelled into space
S olt went with him, making a disgrace
T he planet they went to was full of glowing peanuts
R ow after row making smiley faces
O n a planet that no one knows
N ow Solt made a big mistake
A ccidentally putting dust on the peanuts, making them pepper
U nfortunately, everything turned into cheese
T urning the planet around into a cheesy *bomb*.

Martha Brown (8)
St Charles' Catholic Primary School, Spennymoor

Your Own World

Take a minute to close your eyes,
Look up high in the sky.
Dream of fairy tales and butterflies,
I believe that you can fly.
Wander off into your own wonderland,
With cats and dogs,
I will take your hand.
Bring some logs,
Fetch some sticks,
Let's have a campfire!
Now, you have lots to pick!
All the food you could ever desire,
But be quick, time's nearly up,
Pack your things and prepare for a long flight.
Back down into bed, a yawn and stretch and we're back!

Sophie Emm (10)
St Charles' Catholic Primary School, Spennymoor

Football

Football, I hope I don't fall aiming for the goal,
Aiming for the goal with my heart and soul,
Tried to pass,
Doing everything I learned in class,
Moving so fast,
It's almost half-time,
To miss will be a crime,
I fell on the grass,
Because I missed the pass,
The whistle blew,
So I went to see my Grandma Sue,
I will practise until dinner,
Because in football I am always a winner!

Amalie Wilkinson
St Charles' Catholic Primary School, Spennymoor

Pirate Peter

There was an old pirate called Peter
His favourite food was fajitas
His boat was called Express
It was always a mess
He used a sword when he was fighting
He could run as fast as lightning.

He used to look for treasure
It gave him lots of pleasure
He used a map to look for gold
The things he found were very old
People used to hunt him down
You will never see him frown.

Jack Robinson (8)
St Charles' Catholic Primary School, Spennymoor

Dreaming About Dinosaurs

D reaming about dinosaurs
I guanodon jumping through the grass
N edoceratops charging like a bull!
O viraptors and their protective mouth
S pinosaurus and its large spine,
A rgentinosaurus the largest dinosaur alive
U tahraptor running miles and miles
R ajasaurus roaring like a lion
S uchomimus swimming in the seas, as cool as can be!

Kian Arnott (10)
St Charles' Catholic Primary School, Spennymoor

Scary Dreams

There was a little girl called Bella who lost her way
Who thought that she could not get out of the forest
by the end of the day.

The sky was getting darker
Which made finding her way harder.

She ran and ran until she tripped and fell
None of this was going well.

She rolled and rolled until she landed in a stream
To then wake up to realise it was just a dream.

Isla Taylor (9)
St Charles' Catholic Primary School, Spennymoor

Once Upon A Dream

Once upon a dream
I would zoom into space on a spaceship
I would score a goal every time
I would go on a forever, forever Ferris wheel.

Once upon a dream
I would pick delicious chocolate off Christmas trees
I would live in sunny Menorca
I would catch a fish underneath a waterfall.

Once upon a dream
I think it's time for bed...!

William McMullan (7)
St Charles' Catholic Primary School, Spennymoor

The Dream

When I had a dream I shut my eyes
I was in space
And I could fly
I could breathe in space
And that's no lie
I can't believe I could actually fly
I saw a black hole
And in space it was quiet and cold
Then I saw a rocket so I said hi
But then it left so I said goodbye
I waited a while until I opened my eyes
It was just a dream!

Vinny Baker (9)
St Charles' Catholic Primary School, Spennymoor

My Dreams

At night-time in my dreams, I dream of school and all those things
Pen and paper, books and maths
I dream of all those awesome tasks
Football, hula-hoop and skipping ropes
I even dream of our Pope
Friends are few and far between
Especially when they treat me like a queen
Art and English I like to do
But I also like ICT too!

Eryn Turner (9)
St Charles' Catholic Primary School, Spennymoor

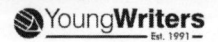

My Pony Velvet

On a bright sunny day
We make our way
To the fields all green and grassy
Where my pony turns a little bit sassy
She cocks her tail and flicks her mane
I hope she always stays the same
She makes me laugh
When I give her a bath
I tickle her tum
And she itches her bum
I hope we'll always have so much fun.

Summer (8)
St Charles' Catholic Primary School, Spennymoor

Once Upon A Dream In Fairy Tale Land

The unicorns shimmer in the darkness,
When they gallop wildly through the enchanted forest.

The fairies leap in the flowers,
When they dance prettily through the enchanted forest.

The butterflies flutter in the beautifulness,
When they move quickly through the enchanted forest.

All my wonderful dreams.

Heidi Scott (8)
St Charles' Catholic Primary School, Spennymoor

Flower Land

In my dreams every night,
Flowers I see upon the light,
Butterfly friends fly across the wind,
With their flattering wings.

One by one, they pass me by,
In the shiny, sparkling sky,
Every night, I leave flowers, hoping they stay but they just disappear,
For now, hopefully next year they will reappear.

Romany Lockwood (8)
St Charles' Catholic Primary School, Spennymoor

Counting Sheep

As I closed my eyes,
The sheep appeared before me,
Jumping one by one,
And the baby cattle murmuring beside them.
I counted them one by one,
I glanced over my shoulder,
To see I was on a farm,
But the wind started to get colder,
Then I opened my eyes,
But to my surprise,
I was in bed.

Emilia Beston (7)
St Charles' Catholic Primary School, Spennymoor

Dancer

D reaming amid the moonlit mirrors,
A rrabella prances and pivots until she shivers,
N ever imagining her dreams could come true,
C ommitment carried her passions to come through,
E xtraordinary, like she was floating on air,
R emarkable rhythm helps highlight her flair.

Amelia Wade (9)
St Charles' Catholic Primary School, Spennymoor

Playing In The Premier League

F antastic feet of a young boy
O ver this side and that side
O nly making one mistake
T aking the ball around the defence
B all skills were immense
A lways a team player, a manager's dream
L eading his team to victory
L eague winners of 2024.

Callum Brown (11)
St Charles' Catholic Primary School, Spennymoor

The Day I Was Born

The day I was born there were giants
They stood smiling softly at me
Saying, "Aww, she is so cute"
They said, "She will like playing in the mud"
Next the giants didn't seem big at all
I got taller and I realised they were my mum and dad
One day I will be a giant to somebody.

Larna McLeod (8)
St Charles' Catholic Primary School, Spennymoor

The Red Dragon

The scaly red dragon flying through the air
In a gust of thunder
A fire was there.

The apple tree sat there until
The apples fell off
And onto the dragon's head with a plop.

The dragon looked around
And saw the wolf with a branch in its mouth
Shaking the apples off.

Finlay Hodgson (11)
St Charles' Catholic Primary School, Spennymoor

The Snake And The Eagle

As I slip through rocks, eagles glide,
As I hunt for mice, eagles hunt for me,
I need to be careful or they will feast on me.

My scales shine as the sun shines,
So bright that I wish it was moonlight.

Slithering and sliding,
Faster and faster I go,
I see a crack and in I go.

Harry Glasper (8)
St Charles' Catholic Primary School, Spennymoor

Terror

T he wizard and I were on our ship
E dging across the ocean when a
R attling sound came from a cupboard on deck
R ipping waves smashed our ship, but luckily
O verhead was a beautiful pirates's dragon to
R escue us as a monster burst from the cupboard.

Harry Machin (10)
St Charles' Catholic Primary School, Spennymoor

In Dreams

In dreams, you can fly
In dreams, you can touch the sky
In dreams, you can see a dinosaur
In dreams, you can lie on the grass
In dreams, you can be on a swing
But some dreams are bad
Even terrible
But don't worry, I'll be there too
I'll explore with you.

Emma Foster (8)
St Charles' Catholic Primary School, Spennymoor

Goodison Park

Me and my dad went to Goodison Park,
We didn't get home until it was dark.

I went to Goodison Park,
My dad met Mark.

I went to Goodison Park,
And I saw a scary shark.

I went to Goodison Park,
I saw Jack Clarke.

I love Goodison Park.

Carter Barratt (7)
St Charles' Catholic Primary School, Spennymoor

Football

F ootball stadium full of supporters
O vercrowded
O verjoyed
T he crowds are cheering
B all is shot into the top corner
A nd crowds go wild
L eft foot into the net
L ove it! One-nil to Man City.

Joel Brown (10)
St Charles' Catholic Primary School, Spennymoor

Mascot

M y head was so happy and excited
A ll my dreams had come true
S t James' Park was the venue
C heering on the players, the roar was so loud
O ut I walked from the tunnel
T he mascot for my team, Newcastle United.

Isaac Ramsay (7)
St Charles' Catholic Primary School, Spennymoor

The War Body

One day I woke up as the bombs lit up the sky,
And I wiped tears from my eyes,
Noise made me cry as I went down to lie,
I looked up at the night sky,
And wondered why, oh why?
As I opened the door I didn't know if I was going to live or die.

William Armstrong (9)
St Charles' Catholic Primary School, Spennymoor

Clowns

C lowns in my lovely dream overwhelmed
L oyalty blesses me in this forsaken world
O n a royal throne
W atching as clowns have me thrown
N ever-ending pain
S uddenly my dream ended and relief remained.

Jake Lim (9)
St Charles' Catholic Primary School, Spennymoor

Virtual Life

I couldn't believe it,
I finally got my VR headset,
Which I didn't think I'd get,
So I connected it straight to the net,
As I turned on the screen,
It looked so colourful and green,
I felt like I was in the best dream!

Seb Connor Inchliffe (9)
St Charles' Catholic Primary School, Spennymoor

Spiders

S piders creep around
P ut them outside
I nside, you're not safe
D o you like spiders?
E ight hairy legs they have
R oaming around in small spaces
S pinning silky webs.

Bertie Corner (8)
St Charles' Catholic Primary School, Spennymoor

The Night Sky

Wonderful stars shine bright in the midnight light
Sparkling and shining
Through the beautiful starlight
The trees swaying on a windy night
Blowing the leaves left and right
The moon is shining oh-so bright.

Sophie-Nicole Hocking (9)
St Charles' Catholic Primary School, Spennymoor

On The Sunny Fields With A Horse

On the sunny fields, it was,
Just me and my horse,
I found a fly so,
I told it to back off,
Until my horse chucked me off,
I was scared,
And I was lonely,
Until I found something to do.

Isla Barton (8)
St Charles' Catholic Primary School, Spennymoor

Police Are Aware

P rotecting people from crime
O ffences that need to be stopped
L ost somewhere or missing
I nteresting work to do
C ustody for offences
E xciting jobs done.

Joseph Hall (9)
St Charles' Catholic Primary School, Spennymoor

Once Upon A Book

I'm stuck in a book,
What's with my look?
Pictures and photographs,
Words and chapters.
Dragons and unicorns,
Giants and lions,
Are following me,
And will have me for tea.

Harris Granger (8)
St Charles' Catholic Primary School, Spennymoor

Roller Skating Competition

I skate fast and snappy
It makes me happy

My skating is amazing
I am always concentrating

When I was done
The judge said I had won.

Freya Barratt (7)
St Charles' Catholic Primary School, Spennymoor

Twinkle Sprinkle Little Fairy

In and out the fairy goes,
Twinkle sprinkle little fairy,
Make the worry disappear.
A little girl fast asleep, worried about a race.
The fairy appears and gives her a dream,
In her dream she is full of pace.
Twinkle sprinkle little fairy,
A little boy lay in bed.
"I'm scared of tomorrow's quiz," he said.
Twinkle sprinkle little fairy,
Sprinkled some dust to help his worry.
Determined he was to win the quiz,
He fell asleep with much ease.
My fairy visits everyone,
Worry and grief are all gone.
They'll feel much better when they wake
Tomorrow is a brand new day to make
Twinkle sprinkle little fairy,
Make the worry disappear.

Khadeeja Laheri (7)
Winston Way Academy, Ilford

My Magical Dream

When I dream every night,
I always see a sparkly light.
Unicorns fly way up high,
Creating a colourful rainbow in the sky.
Their wings move swift and slow,
As they perform their wonderful show.

In the distance I can see,
A joyful village there will be.
The fairies are busy working,
As there is a festival coming.
The children will always play,
When I come, they have lots of stories to say.

We all have fun and flutter everywhere,
But suddenly a sound, which we all could hear.
The fairies and unicorns insist we stay,
But I have to say, another day.
After all the goodbyes are said,
I wake up and see myself still in bed.

Ashika Ray (11)
Winston Way Academy, Ilford

The Unknown Tale Of Dream

In realms unknown, a poem takes flight,
Unheard by others, a hidden delight.
With words unseen, it dances and gleams,
A secret gem, beyond all extremes.
Whispers of verses, like a gentle breeze,
Caress the soul, with a tender ease.
Unveiling thoughts, in a unique way,
A treasure discovered, this very day.
In silence it thrives, this poem untold,
A masterpiece rare, yet to unfold.
May it touch your heart, in its own way,
A hidden gem, to brighten your day.
For dreams are the fuel that ignite our soul,
Guiding us forward towards our goal.
In this hidden gem, dreams find their place,
A source of inspiration, a saving grace.

Aysha Hassan (8)
Winston Way Academy, Ilford

Dinosaur Dreams

Dinosaurs stood in every corner,
It would make you think you were a goner.
Some of them ruled the land,
While also acting very grand.
A few supervised the vast blue sky,
Eating anything passing by.
Everyone was acting as they should be,
Suddenly, one started chasing me.
I ran for my life,
Then one from the sky made a huge dive.
In the blink of an eye, they had a vicious fight,
Which they fought with all their might.
One fell down with a thud,
Which splattered a lot of mud.
At this terrible sight, I closed my eyes with dread,
And soon I realised I was safe at home, in my bed!

Riyansh Yadav (9)
Winston Way Academy, Ilford

Night, Come Back!

Now that the night is gone, I miss the dark night
Now that the only thing left is blinding light
And it's something else, neither night nor day
Maybe everyone is happy that they cheer hooray!

But I miss the night because you rest after a tiring day
When it is dark is when I best see the dreams my way
Maybe it has become a bit too bright
I once thought dark was creepy compared to light
But it is the time when the stars are alight

The dreams once embraced me
Now that it's gone, I really miss the calm
Now that the only thing left is light
So please come back, night!

Zara Mansoor (8)
Winston Way Academy, Ilford

The Christmas Miracle

Santa came from the chimney
With his big, fat tummy
The reindeer ate their carrots
Snowflakes flared just like barite
The children were in deep sleep
It was cold and the night was deep
The Christmas tree dazzled as always
Angels, bells and stockings hung in the doorway
Snowmen as white as paper
Candlelit carols by the choir appeared greater
Gingerbread house looked amazing
Sugar cookies and decorations had Santa gazing
Santa left the best gifts around the tree
Presents on Christmas morning made kids happy
Ho, ho, ho, it's fun surprises, smiles and a joy-filled Christmas.

Bhavyesh Bejjam (9)
Winston Way Academy, Ilford

We Have Dreams

All around me is dark that I see
But far away is colour I see
When I close my eyes,
I see a field of butterflies.

I climb a mountain higher and higher.
When I reach the end, on a corner, I see a spider.
Its eight legs dancing a surprising sight,
Adding a twist to my adventurous flight.

The colours and creatures, they come alive.
In my imagination, where dreams thrive.
With every step, a new world unfolds,
Where stories are written and tales are told.

So, let's keep exploring, my friend, you and I,
On this poetic journey, where imagination can fly.

Soraiya Abul (9)
Winston Way Academy, Ilford

Hogwarts The Wizard School

Harry Potter and I will learn spells together and be the best wizards in the school.

We'll make a group called 'Izards By Wizards.'

Then, we'll fly high in the sky with our broomsticks under us,

We'll have some fun together.

I would like to have a fire dragon as my pet

I will have my own wand and go on magical adventures with my fire dragon and Harry Potter.

Together we will fight villains if they do something bad or get in our way

Then we'll try to become the best wizards in the whole wide world!

Yeshmith Chandanam (8)
Winston Way Academy, Ilford

Sonic Speed

I am running at sonic speed,
In a sprinting race, in the lead.
My extra fast sonic feet,
Hit the ground with a beat.
Person by person, I pass them by,
Everyone thinks that this is a lie.

This is a wonderful superpower,
Others are getting slower and slower.
I have now finished first,
With a quick lightspeed burst.
I always tell them that it's true,
But they go away like they flew.
Later, they really believe me,
Now, I am at home drinking tea.

I realise it's a dream,
On my face, I had a beam.

Shashank Yada (9)
Winston Way Academy, Ilford

The Beach

In my dreams every night,
The waves on the beach go splish and splosh,
Going up and down,
Children screaming and shouting everywhere,
While parents see the waves going up and down,
I just sit there building sandcastles,
All the children rushing to get ice cream with their parents,
While the waves splish and splosh,
After coming back the children scream and shout again,
While I sit being relaxed and calm,
When it grows dark everyone goes,
And when I wake up, I'm all comfy in bed.

Jarin Khan (7)
Winston Way Academy, Ilford

Nightmares And Getting Lost

One night I woke up at five,
Tossing and turning all night,
I woke out of my bed,
Spinning my head,
I felt as if my stomach dropped out of my body,
I tiptoed out of my room,
As soon as I reached the bathroom door I fell,
Into a world that seemed like an underworld,
Then a dark shadow-like man chased me from left to right and side by side,
I covered myself in a blanket in fright and held tight,
I opened my eyes and to my delight,
I saw the day of light,
Was it a dream?

Juhanah Islam (8)
Winston Way Academy, Ilford

The Spring Magical World

On the spring magical world,
There was a bunny coming faster,
Faster, faster, faster, faster,
Than a big wild cat.

On this spring magical world,
There was an elephant face,
Like a lion,
And their wings are bigger,
Bigger, bigger than an ostrich's,
And in the way I saw Harry Potter,
Ron and Hermione.

On the spring magical world,
I saw all human faces,
Like tigers and faster,
Faster, faster than anything.

Hithesh Chigichorla (8)
Winston Way Academy, Ilford

Football

F irst, I found myself on a huge pitch,
O h my god, it's bigger than I imagined!
O n my way towards the pitch, the fans started shouting,
T he coach started cheering me on,
B efore the referee blew the whistle I looked up and there were so many people!
A fter the whistle blew I was quite scared,
L ooking around I felt really lucky,
L uckily I woke up before my emotions started to kick in.

Yannis Chira (9)
Winston Way Academy, Ilford

The Firedrake

The Firedrake who has horns,
When birds and beasts are born,
He soared up to the sky,
Being very shy,
He shot fire out of his mouth,
As he travelled south,
Into Dwarfland,
He cleared sand and dust,
Having a fire lust face,
He dragged his body into a mountain,
And looked at a golden fountain,
As greed overtook him,
He swung his limb,
Boom!
The mountain opening was closed,
As he dozed.

Arjun Selvamariappan (10)
Winston Way Academy, Ilford

Superhero

S ometimes, I get confused what's inside me!
U sually, I don't dream, but now it's different!
P owerful me! Is ready to save the world,
E arth is now my responsibility,
R est, all is fake reality!
H ero, the superhero! Inside me wants to know!
E verything, every night is why, dissimilar to me!
R elax! And dream again!
O nly I can feel that pain!

Ranveer Singh (11)
Winston Way Academy, Ilford

Fairy Story

I went into the woods one day,
And there I walked and lost my way,
When it was so dark that I could not see,
A little creature came to me,
He said if I would sing a song,
The time would be long,
But first, I will have to give him my hand tight
Or else the wood would give me a fright,
I sang a song, he let me go
But now I'm home again but there's no one I know.

Haram Bhatti (9)
Winston Way Academy, Ilford

My Paradise

I dream I'm somewhere nice,
With a book in hand and a glass filled with ice.

I dream I'm somewhere hot,
With warm steamy food in a pot.

I don't want to be woken from this dream,
Or else I'm going to be filled with anger and with steam.

When the time is right I will wake up in delight,
When I wake up from dreaming I can feel my face beaming.

Gabrielle Jones-Fletcher (8)
Winston Way Academy, Ilford

Ayaana's Poem

My name is Ayaana,
And I am eight years old,
I like the warm summer weather,
But I don't like the winter cold,
I like to eat sushi,
As that's my favourite food,
If you haven't already tried it,
Then you need to try it, dude!
I am kind and caring,
And I am always sharing,
I like to read books,
And I want to learn how to cook.

Ayaana Alom (8)
Winston Way Academy, Ilford

A Lake Of Dreams

Bright blue water along the grass,
Ducks that glow and boats that row,
Frogs that are green and leaves that flow along a moat,
A boat that is going as far as it can go.

I look up to the bright sun and think of a dove,
Why a dove?
Why a dove you might say,
Well, because it flies high to give the moon my lake of dreams.

Aanika Momi (9)
Winston Way Academy, Ilford

A Lovely Dream

In your little dream,
You could see amazing things like a starlight beam,
Maybe a unicorn,
Dancing in a field full of corn,
Perhaps fairies having fun,
Whilst singing, "Dun, dun, dun, dun,"
In your dreams, there are several things to see,
But only if it's meant to be.

Zara Ali (9)
Winston Way Academy, Ilford

A Boy In Space

Outer space is where I really like to go,
I ride inside a spaceship, don't you know,
I like to travel through the stars,
And waving at Jupiter and Mars,
Outer space is my favourite place to go.
I didn't want to go back to Earth,
I wanted to be just right, on the moon forever!

Hem Suryansh Kalapala (7)
Winston Way Academy, Ilford

The Perfect Sunset

In twilight grass, the day retires,
As stars ignite their distant fires,
The moon ascends with silver grace,
Casting shadows on nature's face.
A river weaves a liquid song,
Meandering swift and strong.
Moutains rise with ancient pride,
Peaks in Heaven's touch reside.

Zuhaib Hassan (9)
Winston Way Academy, Ilford

Magical Horses

In my dreams every night,
Magical horses come to excite,
Moonlit paths and moonbeam manes,
Dancing in the stormy rains,
With the colourful, longest, sparkling tails,
The horses leave the deepest trails,
I look into the blue and windy sky,
Seeing the magical horses fly.

Shriya Deshpande (10)
Winston Way Academy, Ilford

Astronaut

I am an astronaut
I like doughnuts
I am going to the moon
Very soon
I fly in the sky
I meet stars in my car
I am very happy
And parties I dream of every night
With flying colours
So bright,
I meet rainbows with my little sparrow in.

Siddhi Gannu (8)
Winston Way Academy, Ilford

Lost Boys And Girls

In my dreams every night,
Space boys and girls,
Lost in thin light,
They were ever so bright,
Now they are out of sight,
Wonder when they will be back,
They are missed ever so much,
Just want to feel their touch.

Amira Islam (8)
Winston Way Academy, Ilford

Rich Money

When I lived in France near the Eiffel Tower,
I was watching TV until they said the lottery numbers and I won!
I was excited, proud and happy.
I got VIP tickets to meet Usain Bolt.
We owned three houses and a PlayStation 5.

Rayan Mohammed (7)
Winston Way Academy, Ilford

The Clear River In My Dream

In my dreams I see clear rivers embrace life and dance free,
Its gentle currents caress each tree,
From the mountain top to the sea,
Its journey flows a liquid symphony,
Where serenity grows.

Alessia Maria (9)
Winston Way Academy, Ilford

YOUNG WRITERS INFORMATION

We hope you have enjoyed reading this book – and that you will continue to in the coming years.

If you're a young writer who enjoys reading and creative writing, or the parent of an enthusiastic poet or story writer, do visit our website **www.youngwriters.co.uk**. Here you will find free competitions, workshops and games, as well as recommended reads, a poetry glossary and our blog.

If you would like to order further copies of this book, or any of our other titles, then please give us a call or visit **www.youngwriters.co.uk**.

Young Writers
Remus House
Coltsfoot Drive
Peterborough
PE2 9BF
(01733) 890066
info@youngwriters.co.uk

YoungWritersUK   **YoungWritersCW**
youngwriterscw   **youngwriterscw**